# OLD TE  I

## Andrew Emmerson

SHIRE PUBLICATIONS

Published by Shire Publications Ltd,
PO Box 883, Oxford, OX1 9PL, UK
PO Box 3985, New York, NY 10185-3985, USA
Email: shire@shirebooks.co.uk    www.shirebooks.co.uk

© 2009 Andrew Emmerson.

First published 2009.
Transferred to digital print on demand 2016.

Every attempt has been made by the Publishers to secure
the appropriate permissions for materials reproduced in
this book. If there has been any oversight we will be happy
to rectify the situation and a written submission should be
made to the Publishers.

A CIP catalogue record for this book is available from the
British Library.

Shire Library no. 337  •  ISBN-13: 978 0 7478 0732 2

Andrew Emmerson has asserted his right under the
Copyright, Designs and Patents Act, 1988, to be identified
as the author of this book.

Designed by Ken Vail Graphic Design, Cambridge, UK.
Typeset in Perpetua and Gill Sans.

Printed and bound in Great Britain.

**Cover image**
Demonstrating a brand-new television set in the mid
1950s. In those days televisions were proper pieces of
furniture and destined to become the focal point of the
living room. The pattern seen on the screen, known as
Test Card C, was transmitted before the main programmes
started and was accompanied at most times by tuneful
music. In this way viewers could check the picture and
sound quality of their sets.

**Title page image**
The transmitting aerials at Alexandra Palace in north
London are one of the most enduring images of early
television. The strange spiky shape of the top of the tower
became a symbol of television and was seen nightly in the
opening sequence of Television Newsreel for many years.

**Contents page image**
A recurring image of the 1950s was Test Card C,
transmitted for long periods during the day to the
accompaniment of light music. With virtually no daytime
programming, this was all that would be seen on both
channels during the morning and afternoon. The various
geometric patterns allowed engineers installing new
television sets to adjust the picture for best focus and
correct appearance, while the picture and music were
also handy for in-store demonstrations.

**Acknowledgements**

Thanks are due to all who contributed so willingly with help
and information, particularly for illustrations supplied by:

3M Ltd, page 34; Mike Bennett, pages 20 (bottom), 21
(top), 22 (right), 23 (top), 28 (bottom), 37, and 46 (top
right); BT Archives, title page; Hugh Cocks, page 41 (top);
Andrew Henderson, pages 5, 6 (bottom), 8, 9, 10, 11, 14
(bottom left), 16 (bottom), 17 (left), 24, 26 (top), 27
(top), 42, and 52; Ray Herbert, page 7 (both); Jonathan
Hill, pages 21 (bottom right), and 33 (bottom left); Dicky
Howett, page 14 (bottom right); Jeremy Jago, page 32
(top); Steve James, page 46 (bottom); Bernard King, page
6 (top right); Steve Ostler, pages 4, 15 (top), and 47 (top),
and Reed Business Publishing Ltd, cover image.

Shire Publications is supporting the Woodland Trust, the UK's leading woodland conservation charity, by funding the dedication of trees.

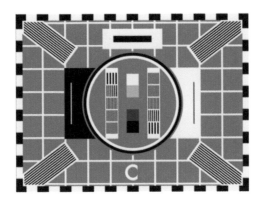

# CONTENTS

# INTRODUCTION

Television has been called the 'magic box' and there is much interest in how this medium of global information and entertainment began as a technical curiosity, became a novelty for the well-off and has finally become a device that is found in almost every home. This book provides a handy guide to television in the home and to how the programmes were viewed from the time television began until the 1980s.

Despite its up-to-the-minute nature, television has reached a ripe old age and in most countries public television broadcasting has been going for well over half a century. This may be why old television receivers, programmes and ephemera – the tangible heritage of the golden age of black and white television – are today attracting a level of interest never previously seen. This book will help put past and present into context and shed a light on how it all developed.

Deciding what constitutes 'old' television is a matter of opinion but for the purposes of this book our cut-off point is the 1980s, at the beginning of the home video and satellite age. It does not matter whether your first television memories are from the 1980s, the Coronation broadcast of 1953 or even the pioneering programmes of the pre-war era. Anyone who shares an interest in the television of the past should enjoy this book.

Right: A collector's dream? Mirror-lid sets from the 1930s can still be found but frequently require much restoration to make them work or look as good as this example. They are also extremely heavy and take up a lot of room.

# THE EARLIEST DAYS
# OF TELEVISION

TELEVISION TODAY is an up-to-the-minute medium, particularly in this age of global satellite broadcasting and the imminent advent of digital pictures with high definition. The technology of television, on the other hand, already has a rich and colourful past reaching back to the 1920s.

Like sound radio, television cannot be claimed as the invention of any one individual; numerous experimenters contributed ideas and improvements to the technology of bringing moving pictures with sound into the home.

How far does television go back? As a concept, it had been discussed by scientists since before the First World War and from the late 1920s onwards experimenters in several countries had demonstrated live television of sorts. It was television, but not as we know it today.

Wise brains wondered if television would ever be more than a novelty. The fourteenth edition of *Encyclopaedia Britannica*, published in 1929, asserted that 'many technical problems have yet to be solved before television can claim to be more than an interesting novelty.'

Then television worked best in people's imagination – on the cinema screen. The videophone had already made its debut in the 1929 German film *Metropolis* and indeed, shortly after, real-life video telephone services were put into commercial use in Germany and France. To judge by films such as *Radio Parade of 1935*, live colour television was already a

Great was the excitement when television broadcasts began in 1936. Although few people could afford the sets, this did not stop them wanting to read about the subject.

5

Top left: 'Oh, you're wasting your time with wireless – the thing now is television!' Television was a ready inspiration for humour in the 1930s.

THE GRAPHIC, FEBRUARY 28, 1925

Top right: John Logie Baird is often called the 'father of television', although the electronic television systems of today have little to do with the electromechanical techniques he employed in the late 1920s and early 1930s. His most significant contribution was to develop public awareness of television. This superb quarter-scale model of a Baird Televisor set was made by Bernard King. Visible on the right is the viewing window, while the circular casing at the rear covered the scanning disc, which rotated at 750 rpm.

Right: On 28 February 1925 *The Graphic*, a weekly newspaper, reported Baird's success in demonstrating television. The article concluded: 'At present the invention is in its infancy, but already it is possible to note the person at the transmitting end winking or opening his mouth – a distinct advance.'

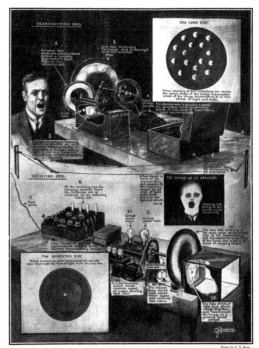

A SUCCESSFUL ATTEMPT TO SEE BY WIRELESS

reality in Britain and, even if not, the public were convinced it was not far around the corner. Another film that confidently proclaimed the use of television in a totally matter-of-fact way was *The Tunnel*, a barely remembered science fiction epic, also from 1935, which imagined the successful completion not of the Channel Tunnel but of a transatlantic tunnel linking Britain to the United States. And an advertising film of 1934, *Plenty of Time for Play*, portrayed a vision of life in twenty years time, including a credible simulation of large-screen television.

It was also clear that a section of the public still had some very strange ideas – and only a hazy comprehension of the capabilities of television. The American film *Death by Television*, also from 1935, was a 'schlock horror' movie about a businessman assassinated by television death rays, but this was in America, where filmgoers believed that anything could happen.

The first person to exploit television commercially was the Scottish inventor John Logie Baird, starting in 1925. He used an electromechanical system to scan images for transmission; a rotating disc about 18 inches across and pierced with holes in a spiral produced a picture made up of thirty 'slices' or lines (these were vertical, unlike the horizontal scanning system of today). The persistence of human vision meant that viewers saw a complete picture, the viewing device being a neon lamp in front of which rotated another disc pierced with holes. By keeping the transmitting and receiving discs in synchronism, viewers could see over a radio link (or by closed circuit wires) an exact replica of the transmitted scene.

Although the pictures were somewhat flickery and no larger than a postcard, they were true moving pictures and the broadcasts could be received over much of Britain (and sometimes on the Continent, too). From 1929 to 1935 television programmes were transmitted by the BBC on the Baird thirty-line system and it would be wrong to belittle this achievement. Nonetheless, despite many improvements, the electromechanical system was inflexible and was no match for the more versatile electronic method of television that was to follow.

Below left: In the Baird system images were scanned vertically, whereas modern television pictures are composed of horizontal lines. The scanning lines are visible in this photograph, which also shows the remarkable picture quality for a system employing only thirty 'slices' or lines.

Below right: Television equipment of the electromechanical era tends to have a Heath Robinson air, an impression that this photograph taken in 1934 does nothing to dispel. In this experimental studio are mirror-drum transmitters for thirty- and sixty-line pictures – note the reflectors for the many light bulbs needed to illuminate the subject being televised, also the 'spinning disc' receiver on the shelf at upper right.

As events transpired, the techniques devised by John Logie Baird were to have next to nothing to do with the television system we watch today. A more significant milestone in television history was the start of regular transmissions of all-electronic television, devised by a team of engineers from EMI Ltd led by Isaac Shoenberg. The first regular broadcast took place in 1936.

In this kind of television the scanning is done electronically by deflecting a beam of electrons, both in the pick-up tube of the camera and within the cathode-ray tube of the receiver. The image is built up line by line, transmitted over the airwaves one line at a time, and recreated on the viewing screen in the same way, fifty times a second.

Above: This is the BBC's television control room in 1935, the final year of the Baird scanning system. In the right foreground is a rotating 'Lazy Susan' stand that enabled the engineers to select the caption of their choice.

Right: This magazine cover shows there was much more to a television receiver than the screen.

Far right: The fairy tale of television was certainly magic for manufacturer Kolster-Brands in 1938.

The fundamental principles of television have not changed since 1936 and the only major differences have been improved picture definition (achieved by increasing the number of lines in the television picture) and the enhancement of colour. In Britain, both of these changes were made in the 1960s; 625-line transmissions began in 1964, although the original 405-line signals continued until 1985. Colour, on the Phase Alternate Line (PAL) system, was introduced in 1969.

It is notable that the television heritage that this book celebrates is a genuine British achievement; the world's first electronic television transmissions came from London, using an all-British system devised by engineers from the EMI and Marconi companies. The BBC had the distinction of providing the world's first regular service of entertainment programmes in high definition, as the 405-line service was called in those days. The studios and transmitters at Alexandra Palace in north London were pioneer installations and set the pace for television development the world over in the years to come.

Other countries soon followed suit: France in 1937, Germany in 1938 and the United States in 1939, while just before the war experimental services were starting in Japan, Russia and some other European countries. But it was in Britain where television made the most impact and where

Opposite top right: With the opening of television in 1936 the BBC broke new ground in more ways than one. What were the legal and copyright positions? Nobody was quite sure, so the BBC decided to take no chances by showing this caption.

The BBC's two television studios in the 1930s were quite compact, equipped with a maximum of two cameras of the Emitron pattern.

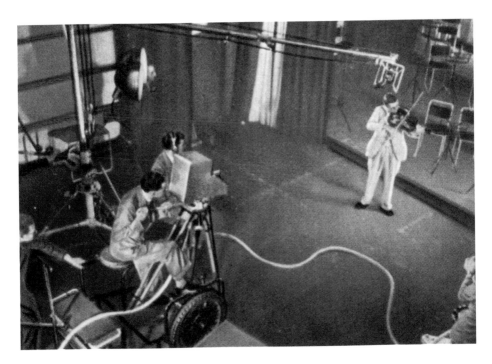

between 1936 and 1939 television programming, entertainment and technology were developed to a remarkable state of completeness.

Although television was seen as a wonder of the age, its social impact was slight in the years from 1936 to 1939. In reality it was a rich person's pleasure, with the least expensive sets costing around £30, six times the average weekly wage. Although some twenty thousand sets were sold, nearly all in the London area, television for most people was a novelty no more affordable than, say, a personal helicopter would be today. All too soon the Second World War brought a reappraisal of broadcasting priorities and all thoughts of television were forgotten for seven years.

That is not to say television had no role to play during the war. Radar equipment borrowed heavily from television circuitry and the production facilities built up before the war for television. The design of the main Chain Home radar transmitters was based on a Baird television transmitter, while an off-the-shelf Pye receiver component design was used in many radar receivers. Even the BBC's television transmitter at Alexandra Palace was pressed into service for 'bending the beams' of hostile radar signals and confusing the enemy.

Inevitably the very first television programmes were studio-bound but it did not take long before the cameras ventured outdoors. The Coronation of 1937 was a landmark outside broadcast and here we see the camera (with rain cover) and some officials at Hyde Park Corner. The blurred passer-by in the foreground does not spoil this candid snapshot.

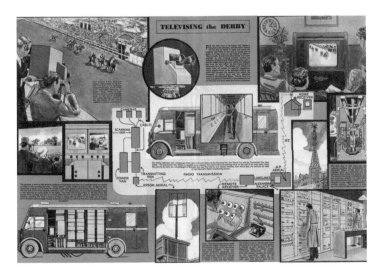

Above: Television made household names (and faces) of its many personalities. One of the most familiar to early viewers was Jasmine Bligh, who introduced television programmes before the war and for a while afterwards. Here she takes the cameraman's viewpoint on one of the Emitron cameras used in those days.

Above: Televising the Derby from Epsom was rightly considered a wonder of the age before the Second World War; until then the only live coverage had been by sound radio, with pictures following in the next day's newspapers or a day or two later in cinema newsreels. Television brought home the event in sight and sound. All the key elements of pre-war television are seen in this drawing: the Emitron camera, the mirror-lid television receiver, the mobile scanner van and the Alexandra Palace aerials.

Below left: The high cost of sets was one of the reasons why television was not a mass entertainment medium before the war. This HMV combined radio and television receiver was one of the cheaper sets, costing 29 guineas (£30 9s.) – around six weeks' average earnings. Very attractively designed and highly sought after today by collectors, it was made in 5-inch and 7-inch screen versions, which meant the picture was watchable only at close distances.

Below right: If money was no object, this artistic Scophony 18-inch screen model might be to your taste. It used a special tube and lenses to project the television image on to a linen screen.

# THE POST-WAR ERA:
# TELEVISION TAKES OFF

THE GROWING PROSPERITY of the 1950s and 1960s made this the period in which television entered nearly everyone's life. For people who grew up in this period, television was probably the most powerful influence, while for the people who made the programmes (and the sets) this black and white era was undoubtedly a golden age of opportunity, creativity and progress.

This was also the era when television first created a broad popular culture of its own. Television became a topic of universal discussion and its images were instantly recognisable – H-shaped aerials appeared on roof tops everywhere and even the little green men from outer space portrayed in newspaper cartoons had an obligatory 'H' antenna grafted on their heads. Television had arrived.

Two factors were responsible for this: rising prosperity, and the Coronation of Queen Elizabeth II. As earnings rose in real terms in the early 1950s, a growing number of people could afford television, especially in the Midlands, where the motor industry and other manufacturing trades were providing good employment and where Britain's second television transmitter had been opened in 1949. Many people took only modest holidays and did not own cars, so television now represented a kind of entertainment and escapism they could afford. To make it easier, rental firms made it possible to buy a set on hire purchase. Gifted individuals built their own receivers from war-surplus radar components.

The televising of the Coronation in 1953 stimulated the sale of sets in two ways. It finally settled the decision many people had been postponing for so long, and those who had to go next door to see the ceremony on their neighbour's set decided afterwards it was time they had a set as well. Two years later, the coming of a second channel, ITV, with its more down-to-earth offering, started a trend for brighter, more popular programmes that was reflected on the BBC as well.

Not everyone was television-minded, though, and for some households the wireless remained the sole source of broadcast entertainment. A few people had difficulty in coming to terms with television altogether. Back in

Opposite:
Many people's fondest memories of old television are of the programmes of their childhood, such as the children's show *Blue Peter*. This photograph, taken in April 1965 at the BBC Television Centre, shows the programme's then presenter, Valerie Singleton. Note the paraphernalia of cameras, cables, lights, cameramen and floor managers.

13

Right: The new regional studios had simpler technical requirements than London. This studio in Bristol demonstrates that almost all that was needed was a camera, a picture monitor, a caption stand and a newsreader (Wynroe Thomas in this case). Note the characteristic four lenses on the camera: these were mounted on a rotary turret and the cameraman chose a focal length appropriate to the shot. Zoom lenses did not become commonplace until the 1970s.

Below: The expansion of television broadcasting in the early 1950s created a ready market for handy guides, in particular this booklet from the *Daily Mail*. Several editions were published and they are both cheap and collectable.

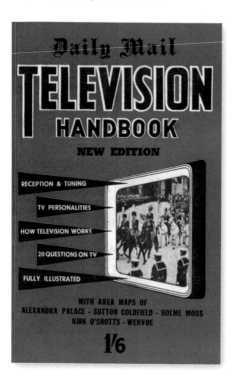

Above right: The demand for more exciting television in the 1950s increased the number of outside broadcasts from events around the country. Reflecting this trend were the Dinky Supertoy productions for fortunate children – these toys were already expensive when new (they were introduced in 1959) and now fetch three-figure sums if well-preserved and in their original boxes. This is the Roving Eye camera vehicle.

The affordable Bush TV22 turned out with a 9-inch screen and a lustrous brown bakelite cabinet. Costing just over £50, this was one of the most successful – and reliable – sets made in the post-war period. Many of these sets are still going today and their collectability has made them highly prized.

1935 the Postmaster General had felt obliged to reassure listeners to BBC radio that television would not be not a two-way process and the set in the living room could not peer into their homes, and this idea that television could watch you while you watched it took some time to die out. Even in the post-war era, one lady in Wakefield, whose habit was to take her bath in front of the fire, did so with towels draped around her so that her TV idol, presenter Macdonald Hobley, could not 'see' her.

An off-screen photograph from the Coronation broadcast of Queen Elizabeth II in 1953. This event, more than any other, brought television into the public consciousness. Many people bought a set specifically to watch the spectacle; those who could not afford to were invited to watch with neighbours.

Left: Another milestone event in British television broadcasting was the start of Independent Television in 1955. Viewers at last had a choice of programming and for the first few months they virtually deserted the BBC.

Below: After the Second World War a number of manufacturers produced some extremely attractive sets, even though few customers could afford them. This is the Baird Countryman model, which had special circuitry to improve reception in poor reception areas.

GUARANTEED
RECEPTION

L A R G E
P I C T U R E

S I M P L E
CONTROLS

P R E - S E T
INTERFERENCE
SUPPRESSION

BAIRD
THE FIRST NAME IN
TELEVISION

Above: Another pervasive fear was that television was some kind of two-way process, as this comic postcard sets out to confirm. In 1935 the Postmaster General had to reassure listeners to BBC radio that the television set in the living room could not peer into their homes.

Above: Some subtle psychology is employed in this poster of the early 1950s to ensure that exultant viewers took out a television licence.

# Pye TV for the
# contemporary home

In strikingly handsome contemporary cabinets designed by world famous Industrial Artist Robin Day, Pye Limited present television receivers of unsurpassed beauty and technical excellence. Each model incorporates Pye 13 Channel Tuning, Automatic Picture Control and Tilted Black Screen for perfect viewing in any light. The Cabinets are finished in either French Walnut or Japanese Sen. 17" Table Model, 79 GNS. tax paid. 17" Console, 87 GNS. tax paid.

*Write to Pye Limited, Box 49 Cambridge for illustrated brochure.*

# THOSE MAGNIFICENT SETS

WHEN television transmissions started in 1936 the sets on sale had a very different appearance from those of today. Because the picture tubes were very long, they were mounted vertically in a cabinet the size of a chest freezer, using a mirror angled at 45 degrees for viewing. These mirror-lid sets, as they are called, were soon supplanted by direct-viewing sets, where you looked in the 'normal' way at a horizontal picture tube, and after the war only one mirror-lid set was produced. Viewers found console (floor-standing) or table sets much more convenient.

Until the mid 1950s, large picture tubes were difficult to make and the only large-screen sets made used a special optical arrangement to project their image on to a linen screen. This produced large pictures, up to 4 feet by 3 feet in size, although these were neither bright nor sharp by today's standards. Further disadvantages were the substantial size (and weight) of these models, comparable to a chest of drawers, and their price – between £120 and £360, at a time when conventional 12-inch sets cost around £70 or £80.

Most homes therefore made do with small screens – 9- and 12-inch tubes were commonplace – meaning that everyone had to crowd around to get a good view. Various magnifying lenses, great bulbous things made of Perspex and filled with paraffin that started off clear and gradually became yellower, were supposed to make the picture look bigger but did not help much.

Magnifying lenses were also required for the home-built sets made in large numbers at this time by enthusiastic amateurs. War-surplus radar parts were available cheaply and magazines published blueprints and instructions to turn these into low-cost television receivers. Dealers sold kits of all the parts necessary, along with simple plywood cabinets. The chief disadvantage was the green screen of the radar tube and its small size; magnifying lenses could enlarge the image but did nothing for the strange hue of the pictures.

What characterised most television receivers made until around 1960 was the quality of their cabinets, styled to match contemporary living-room furniture. Most sets had cabinets clad in high-quality wood veneers and

Opposite: 'Contemporary' styling was the buzzword of late 1950s furniture, and designer Robin Day was the king of contemporary, making Pye Ltd fortunate to acquire his services. It was all about splayed chair legs and Ladderax shelving, both of which feature in this trendy room setting. The looks of the boxy television of 1957 have not aged so well, however.

A display of pre-war television sets by Marconiphone and His Master's Voice, all finished in rich glossy veneers. The table sets seen in the centre offered a choice of a 5-inch or 7-inch round screen and were suitable for smaller rooms. The 9-inch console and mirror-lid sets on either side were intended for more luxurious homes – and needed several people to shift them into place.

some even had tambour or cupboard doors to make them look more like a piece of furniture than a television receiver. Generally the wood was given a high-gloss cellulose finish, often tricked out with 'gold' aluminium trim and 'ivory' plastic knobs with gold inlays. As furniture fashions changed towards more natural-looking veneers, so did television cabinets and by the mid 1960s some very attractive teak and other veneers were being used. At the end of this period some makers adopted the 'pop' look by lacquering sets in white and other startling primary colours, but these were a little too stark for most households.

For cheaper receivers, alternative, less expensive materials had to be found. Some manufacturers (such as Bush and GEC) favoured cases made of polished brown bakelite, a tough but rather brittle plastic material, and these are firm favourites with collectors today, even though they were considered a cheap option in their day. Plywood covered with Rexine (a kind of leathercloth) was the choice for the Ekco TMB270, the first portable combined television/radio (ideal for picnics) and other manufacturers produced both wood and metal cases covered with the same material.

This 21-inch screen sold for 88 guineas, a cunning way of disguising £92 8s. 0d. £6 was a good weekly wage at this time. This set features wobbly wooden legs with brass ferrules for the so-called 'contemporary' look.

Later small sets had cabinets made of plastics such as styrene and polypropylene; these were used on the British-made Perdio Portarama and the imported Japanese Sony TV9-306, both pioneering small-screen transistor portable sets. Full-size sets continued to be made of wood, however.

The introduction of 625-line transmissions in 1964 brought a new technical complication to television receivers – the dual-standard set.

Below left: The space age arrived in 1960 when Sony introduced the world's first all-transistor television. Everything about the set was different: its finish was two-tone grey wrinkle-painted steel, with stainless steel trim, while the adjustable sun visor and clever pull-out-and-twist rod antenna displayed thoughtful industrial design. As befits a design classic, this set can be seen in the Design Museum, London. This model, the TV8-301, was sold in Japan and North America but not in Britain. Sony's first British portable, the TV9-306, followed shortly after but looked far more conventional, with a rather unattractive shiny grey plastic finish.

Below right: Introduced in the 1960s, transistorised sets with lightweight plastic cabinets transformed the way people watched television. This Ultra Cub (also sold under the Ferguson and HMV names) is a typical mid-1960s British-made portable. Released in 1966, it was no lightweight (weighing 15 pounds) and cost 39 guineas (£41 9s. 6d). On the tuner BBC and ITV channels are paired next to one another (1 with 9, 2 with 10, 4 with 8 and so on) to minimise rotary movement when 'turning over' from BBC to ITV.

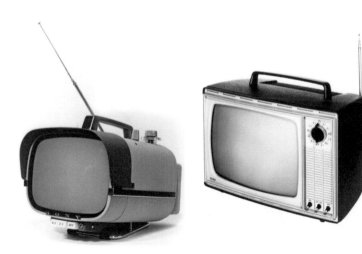

Because the 405- and 625-line systems were so different technically, these new sets amounted to two separate receivers in one cabinet, sharing the same screen and loudspeaker. New sets had to incorporate both systems since it was known that broadcasts on the old 405-line system would be phased out eventually (although in the event it was not until 1985). The launch of colour programmes across all channels in 1969 brought another refinement and some highly involved technology to produce colour pictures. These early colour sets were extremely expensive, physically very heavy and bulky and employed what was then leading-edge technology. Not many were sold initially and most had a fairly short life, being scrapped when more compact (and reliable) colour sets became available. For this reason early colour sets are somewhat rare, although not particularly valuable or collectable.

Nearly all the sets made until the late 1960s used valves. Fundamentally different from the solid-state electronics of today, valves were much bulkier (making sets larger) and generated considerable heat (a source of unreliability). Over time this heat affected other components inside the set, causing control settings to drift. This was one of the reasons why the television companies conveniently broadcast a 'tuning signal' pattern before the start of the afternoon's and evening's programmes – some owners needed time to 'tune in' their sets for the best possible picture. This instability also meant that many sets had more controls on the front panel and some viewers loved fiddling with these until they had what they thought was the perfect picture.

The valves also took several minutes to 'warm up' (older viewers will remember the smell of burning dust coming from inside the set). Some manufacturers dared to turn this 'defect' into an asset – a Pye booklet of around 1949 stated: 'Pye sets take about $2^1/_2$ minutes to warm up after they are switched on. This is because of the very complicated circuits which ensure picture stability. By allowing a longer warming up period, a much greater degree of final stability is achieved.'

*Below right: Colour television experiments had been conducted ever since John Logie Baird began in the late 1920s but it was not until 1955 that the BBC started regular test transmissions (outside normal broadcasting hours). Early receivers were extremely large and cumbersome and, being hand-made prototypes, they were extremely expensive. The only opportunity the public had to see colour television during the 1950s was at special exhibitions.*

*Far right: Colour televisions were extremely expensive in the early 1970s but set makers compensated for this with sleek styling and the use of high-quality veneers of real wood. This Beovision receiver by Bang & Olufsen illustrates the good design of some sets from this era.*

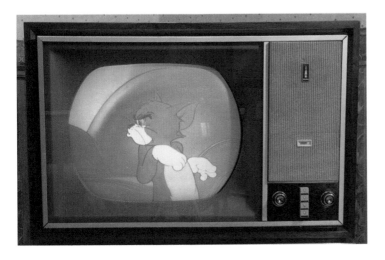

Left: Early colour sets were extremely bulky, as this photo of a British model CVB100 shows. They could easily overpower a small living room and their weight called for a substantial stand too!

Sets were also far less reliable than today, and breakdowns meant that the repair man was a frequent visitor in some households. Such was the unreliability and general uncertainty about the future of television (Independent Television and colour programmes were always rumoured to be 'just around the corner') that many people took the safer option of renting rather than buying their set. The high cost of a replacement picture tube filled many viewers with dread and, in any case, renting was the only option for many households. In those days a television receiver could cost around a sixth of the cost of a small family car, perhaps ten times as much as sets cost today in real terms.

Right: A trade protection agreement initially restricted the Japanese manufacturer Sony to supplying sets with screen sizes of 18 inches and below. Nevertheless, the clear picture on their patented Trinitron screens ensured that Sony had plenty of supporters. Advertisements like this are not made nowadays.

23

# THE FIRST TELEVISION GENERATION

R EPEATS of television programmes from days gone by provide us with an insight into the character of past programmes but give no indication of how they were seen at the time.

Viewing was a shared experience and something of a social event in most households in the 1960s, just as sitting in a circle and listening to the 'wireless' had been before the Second World War. Viewers tended to pay more attention to the programmes than they do today, when some people use television as little more than background distraction. Receivers were neither portable nor cheap, and so any home that had a television set made it the focus of the living room. This effect was emphasised by subdued room lighting, since screens were dimmer than today. It was considered bad for your eyes to watch television in total darkness, so 'tasteful' television lights were sold to provide background illumination. Another essential was a television trolley or table, the latter in the obligatory 'contemporary' style of rich glossy brown wood and tapering splayed legs in black, capped with lacquered brass ferrules.

Optional accessories were decorated leather covers for copies of the *Radio Times* and *TV Times* and stick-on screens that gave a 'lifelike' colour impression to television programmes ('winner of the Brussels Inventors' Fair', no less). At a time when colour television was still no more than a laboratory novelty in Britain, some people were so desperate to have colour television that they bought these garish objects of translucent multicoloured plastic to give their monochrome screens a 'coloured' effect.

Viewing hours were shorter until the early 1960s: a couple of hours around lunchtime perhaps, an hour's children's television from 5 until 6 p.m., and then the 'Toddlers' Truce', when small children were supposed to have their tea and then go to bed. The BBC news at 7 p.m. introduced another three hours' broadcasting, and that was that. The introduction of a second channel, ITV, from 1955 onwards brought in an element of keen competition, which livened up programming and presentation on both channels.

Programmes were introduced by in-vision announcers, and the presentation of captions, weather maps and other ancillary items was less

Opposite:
A mid-1950s advertisement for Rowntree's Fruit Gums. It had no caption or slogan but the message was clear enough – the television age was here.

Right and far right: For many people, buying and watching a television set entailed some sacrifices. Some people paid the rent on their set with a coin-in-the-slot meter, while many saved up for their licence with special stamps bought at the post office.

## "H—! AM I JUST TALKING TO MYSELF?

Right: Television was a natural subject for comic postcards, many of which are highly amusing, but unfit for a family readership. This one is not especially funny but is uncannily accurate in its depiction of television viewing in the 1950s. Note the bulky television receiver and massive armchairs, the velvet pouffe that nobody used and the subdued lighting (to compensate for the none-too-bright television picture).

polished than the sophistication we expect today. Timekeeping on the BBC in particular was more an art than a science and, with most programmes going out live, it was inevitable that sometimes they would overrun, or else finish early. Accordingly, a number of filler items were used when the next programme was not ready to start. People almost looked forward to interlude films of spinning wheels, tropical fish, crashing waves or playful kittens, while the trick photography of the train that raced from London to Brighton in just four minutes was another favourite.

Less welcome were the dreaded captions 'Normal service will be resumed as soon as possible' and 'Do not adjust your set'. The first usually signified that the scheduled programme would be cancelled, since studio breakdowns were by no means uncommon. The second, no more than a catchphrase today but used in earnest during the days of VHF (very high frequency) broadcasting, heralded the dreaded foreign interference that could all but wipe out viewing. The VHF frequencies used were extremely prone to interference from foreign stations when abnormal atmospheric conditions caused transmissions to cover a wider area than usual. Severe patterning on pictures and foreign voices on the sound could reduce viewing enjoyment to zero in the summer months.

Electrical interference was also more pronounced, simply because fewer appliances were fitted with suppressors in those days. Passing cars or a neighbour's vacuum cleaner caused havoc, with patterns and lines all over the picture; the BBC even ran an amusing public information film to alert inconsiderate motorists to the displeasure caused if they did not fit a suppressor.

Television even affected what we ate and the way we ate it. The first signs were innocent enough, when manufacturers started cashing in by selling 'television assortment' tins of biscuits and toffees, but then came the frozen TV dinner, designed to be eaten off a tray while watching *Coronation Street* or the *Sixty-Four Thousand Dollar Question*. Commercials aimed at children

Above left and right: The small dim screens of the 1950s spawned a lively trade in dubious add-ons claimed to enhance the viewer's pleasure. In fact, they served only to fleece an unsuspecting public. The polarised anti-glare filter ('It's dioptric, it's dependable') was supposed to improve picture contrast (not unlike computer monitor filters today), while the colour screen ('It enhances your television viewing') turned your black and white set into a colour one. The clear plastic overlay was tinted blue at the top (for sky), pink in the middle (for flesh tones) and green at the bottom (for grass). Amazingly, some people actually bought these accessories.

27

In the world of television past it is always time for tea. Afterwards perhaps we shall watch Children's Television and we can look in the *Radio Times* to see who is on today.

Below and below right: Today many children have their own television set. So did many children of the 1950s but their personal set was one of these novelty film viewers, which they held to the light to see a few frames of a cartoon film.

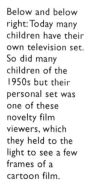

implored 'Don't Forget the Fruit Gums, Mum' or demonstrated the riot-quelling qualities of Nestlé's Milky Bar in the old Wild West. Adults were lured with the charms of Fry's Turkish Delight or were sold such obvious falsehoods as a chocolate bar that could be eaten between meals without ruining the appetite. The era of what sociologists call the 'hidden persuaders' had arrived.

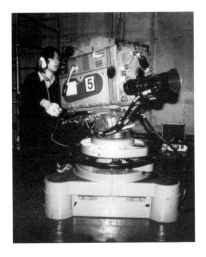

Top left: Many programmes of the past were supremely serene on screen but, just out of vision, the reality in the studio was very different. As late as the mid 1960s shooting television pictures was an energetic job. The cameras and supports were extremely large and cumbersome, yet cameramen manoeuvred them with poise and grace. Full of valves and transformers, the cameras were heavy and hot – very different from the lightweight cameras and solid-state devices of today.

Top right: It is not a strange question that this housewife of 1956 is asking; unsuppressed appliances – and motor vehicles – could ruin television viewing in those days.

Below: The invasion of television culture. The close-up shows a television toffee tin, television money-box, television cigarette lighter, even television egg cups.

**ABC TELEVISION Ltd.**
Midlands
*Saturdays and Sundays*
North of England
*Saturdays and Sundays*

**SOUTHERN TELEVISION Ltd**
Central Southern and
South-East England
*Whole week*

**ANGLIA TELEVISION Ltd.**
East Anglia
*Whole week*

**T W W Ltd.**
South Wales and the
West of England
*Whole week*

**ASSOCIATED-REDIFFUSION Ltd.**
London
*Mondays to Fridays*

**TYNE TEES TELEVISION Lt**
North-East England
*Whole week*

**ASSOCIATED TELEVISION Ltd.**
London
*Saturdays and Sundays*
Midlands
*Mondays to Fridays*

**ULSTER TELEVISION Ltd.**
Northern Ireland
*Whole week*

**BORDER TELEVISION Ltd.**
The Borders
*Whole week*

**WALES (West & North)
TELEVISION Ltd.**
West and North Wales
*Whole week*

**CHANNEL TELEVISION Ltd.**
Channel Islands
*Whole week*

**WESTWARD TELEVISION L**
South-West England
*Whole week*

**GRAMPIAN TELEVISION Ltd.**
North-East Scotland
*Whole week*

**INDEPENDENT TELEVISION
NEWS Ltd.**
Provides the main news
bulletins for all Independ
Television areas

**GRANADA TV NETWORK Ltd.**
North of England
*Mondays to Fridays*

**SCOTTISH TELEVISION Ltd.**
Central Scotland
*Whole week*

**INDEPENDENT TELEVISION
COMPANIES ASSOCIATION**
The Association acts on
behalf of all the Programm
Companies on certain mat
of common interest

# CHANNELS, STATIONS AND IDENTS

Today's television programmes – at least the terrestrial ones – reach us over a classification of airwaves called UHF or ultra-high frequencies. In the black and white era the programmes were broadcast on rather lower frequencies in the VHF (very high frequency) band, also known before the Second World War as the ultra-short wave or USW band.

Before the war there was just one television channel, unnumbered in those days, plus an auxiliary frequency used by the BBC for receiving outside broadcast contributions. In the post-war era the BBC was allocated a total of five channels (1 to 5), designated as Band I. Additional channels in Band III were provided for ITV (and also shared in a few locations by the BBC). These were numbered 6 to 14, although channel 14 was never used. The Republic of Ireland also had a 405-line television service, using some of these channels, and these Irish programmes could be received in parts of Wales and England. There were also plans for offshore 'pirate' television stations in the 1960s but, unlike the radio ships, these never came to fruition.

As television expanded to cover the whole of Britain, additional transmitter stations were erected, often on windswept hills and crags with evocative names. Viewers who searched their atlases for Pontop Pike, North Hessary Tor, Holme Moss and Rumster Forest, for example, did so in vain, however, since the places they referred to were as obscure as the names mentioned in the shipping forecasts on the radio.

With the coming of Independent Television from 1955 onwards came the need to distinguish the separate stations and for each to create a distinct on-screen character. Until then the BBC had not set out to create a strong visual identity but with the advent of ITV everything changed. Each programme contractor now had its own brief jingle or musical 'calling card' as well as a more substantial piece of music played at the start of every day's transmissions. Many of these latter melodies were by composers of high standing; independent stations took themselves quite seriously.

Another brand-new feature was the animated visual identification symbol or 'ident' – a spinning star for Associated-Rediffusion, the 'eyes' of ATV and

Opposite:
Some of these ITV companies from the mid 1960s still survive – but none of the original emblems does. Note the Welsh dragon emblem of the Wales West and North station, which lasted only two years before financial collapse.

31

Test cards and other television graphics have attracted serious interest from design students and others. Echoes of Art Deco style can be seen in this pre-war BBC tuning signal used between programme transmissions.

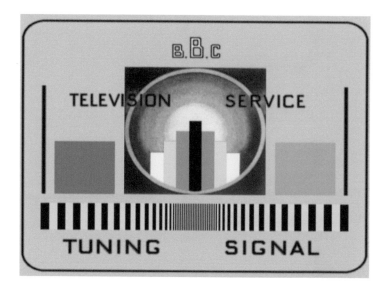

The BBC's 'Television Symbol' of the mid 1950s consisted of two intersecting eyes scanning the globe from north to south and from east to west, supposedly symbolising vision and the power of vision. Flashes of lightning on either side apparently represented electrical forces and the whole form took the shape of wings, which suggested the creative possibilities of television broadcasting.

so on. For its part, the BBC had commissioned an extremely intricate 'Television Symbol', which revolved in an almost impossible fashion between programmes, to the accompaniment of a dainty but not very trendy melody called *Symbol Music* played on the celeste.

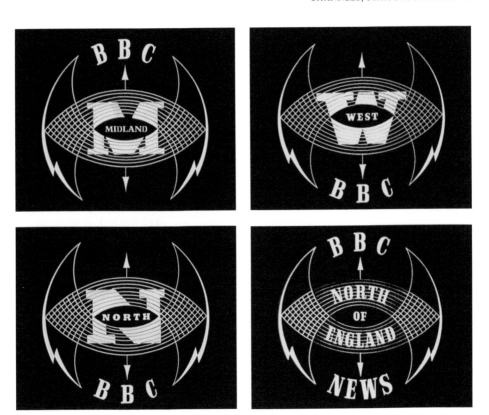

One thing the BBC could not possibly match (to the great relief of many people) was the commercials shown on ITV. Viewers were treated (or subjected) to a remarkable (or mind-numbing) selection of advertising spots, introduced by a variety of starburst animations unique to each station. These owed a lot to contemporary American ideas, so a high proportion made use of cartoon animation and catchy jingles.

Above and below: Some of the long-forgotten regional variations of the on-air BBC ident.

Left: The BBC used the Television Symbol motif with gusto, not only on screen but in publicity material, on canteen crockery and even as a sort of weathervane above the new Wood Lane Television Centre. The symbol's designer was Abram Games, FSIA, a noted commercial artist who also devised the symbol for the 1951 Festival of Britain.

# TAPING TELEVISION

ONE OF THE frustrations of the first fifty years or so of television was its transience. Unless a programme was repeated, there was no way you could enjoy it a second time, which made it very frustrating if you forgot to watch a programme or, worse, your receiver failed (not such an uncommon event, as one of the *Hancock* comedies portrayed so well).

Although the broadcasters had the means to record television programmes, first on film and later on videotape, this ability was not an option for home viewers until the late 1970s, and then only for those with deep pockets. A few people recorded the sound channel of their favourite comedy shows and a handful pointed an 8-mm or 16-mm home movie camera at the television screen but they were the exceptions.

Public expectations were altered in 1963 when the first domestic video recorder was announced. Known as Telcan (canned television), it was demonstrated by the Nottingham Electronic Valve Company with an intended price of £61 19s. Picture quality from this unwieldy machine was described variously as 'barely watchable' or 'appalling', and although the product did eventually reach the market it was not a success.

More manageable but still bulky video recorders were introduced by Philips and Sony in the 1960s. Like the programmes they recorded, they worked in black and white only and used open-reel tape. Schools found them very useful for recording educational programmes but their price (and complexity) discouraged home users.

The first true home video recorder in Britain was the Philips VCR-format machine, the N1500, launched in 1972 (VCR stood for 'video cassette recorder'). The N1500 had the advantage of using cassette tapes but the machine itself was large, temperamental and able to record only 60 minutes maximum. The replacement machine, the N1700 of 1977, managed not only double the playing time but also an improved picture that approached off-air viewing in quality. Priced around £600, these machines were not cheap to buy and those who indulged themselves mainly rented them.

Opposite:
A constant regret is how few television programmes were recorded in the past, and one of the reasons is the size and expense of the equipment needed to make recordings in those days. Here an Ampex 1000 machine is being put through its paces in the BBC research laboratories. These monsters, which were the state of the art around 1960, used tape 2 inches wide. You would not have wanted one of these in your living room.

Smaller videotape machines were on sale by the mid 1960s but these also were far too bulky – and expensive – for domestic viewers. These Peto Scott machines, made by Philips in Holland, sold mainly to schools, colleges and other training establishments.

The dominance of this market by Philips (and 'clone' machines badged with other names) was not to last long. 1977, the year when the VCR-LP machines were introduced, also marked the Japanese invasion of the British home video market. Two rival manufacturer alliances, employing competing (and totally incompatible) tape formats, brought the Beta and VHS systems to the United Kingdom. Neither system produced pictures anywhere near as good as those of the VCR-LP system but they offered up to three (later four) hours' recording time on a smaller and handier tape cassette.

The Beta tape, named after the Greek letter denoting the way the tape passed the recording heads, was invented by Sony, licensed also to manufacturers such as Sanyo and Toshiba and marketed under the names Betamax and Betacord. VHS or 'video home system' was an invention of the Japanese Victor Company, JVC, and made by them, National Panasonic and many other firms (eventually even by Philips after it accepted it had lost the formats war). There was a widespread notion that Betamax machines produced better picture quality than VHS but this was a fiction. The truth was that the Beta system used more aggressive filtering, producing a cleaner picture but with no high resolution. VHS produced more detailed images but at the cost of more 'picture noise' or graininess.

A video recorder was a luxury purchase in 1980 and industry sources record that fewer than four million recorders had been sold by then. At the beginning of the 1980s a VCR machine cost around £700 and you might well have to pay £10 for a blank tape (or three times as much for a pre-recorded film). However, VHS recorders were widely available in rental shops (every high street had

## the important thing about this video tape recorder doesn't show

## its compatibility

True compatibility allowing exchanges of tape between any machines, in a low cost VTR, means a dozen new uses for taped vision. Add in simple operation, input and output circuitry matching studio requirements, the picture quality possible from 3·2 Mc/s bandwidth, up to 60 minutes playing time and automatic sensing of 405 or 625 lines from a compact unit—these are some of the reasons why we claim that the ET 2610 (general purpose) and ET 2770

(studio model) VTR's are outstanding equipment. You'll probably agree when you see the full specification. Both technical information and VTR's are available now.

PETO SCOTT LTD Addlestone Road Weybridge Surrey Tel Weybridge 45511

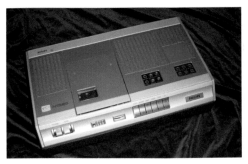

several at that time) and it was this, along with aggressive marketing by manufacturers such as Ferguson, that ensured that the VHS system eventually won the battle of the formats. There was another influence, even if it is seldom recorded. There was no censorship or classification system for 'sell-through' videotapes in the early 1980s, which led to a healthy market in smutty (and tasteful) 'Triple X' movies on tape. These were available widely only on the VHS format and it is no exaggeration to say that the wide availability of rental movies in general, and the film *Deep Throat* in particular, gave home video the kick-start it desperately needed.

Prices fell, picture quality improved and machines became easier to use (stiff piano-key controls soon gave way to soft-touch press buttons). Improvements in videotape manufacturing methods resulted in better-quality pictures and sound, improved reliability and also durability in editing. Within ten years or less a video recorder was in nearly every home. Other improvements in consumer video included extended picture resolution (S-VHS and Super Beta), hi-fi sound and lightweight camcorders in 8-mm, S-VHS and Hi-8 formats.

Above left: The breakthrough came in 1972 with the introduction of a machine that used a convenient tape cassette instead of harder-to-handle open reels. Philips was the inventor of this new system, which they called VCR (although the expression was soon applied to all domestic videotape recorders). This particular machine was an improved model.

Above right: Philips' pre-eminence in the home video market lasted just five years, when its thunder was stolen by the Japanese VHS system. This early 'piano key' model made by JVC was the type of VCR that was bought around 1980. It had no remote control and no fancy features but was a sturdy and reliable machine that soon found a place in many homes.

Right: Cassette formats compared.

# SATELLITE

Number One · Winter 1981 · £1

# TV

## N·E·W·S

RTL

American Forces
Radio &
Television Network
Europe

ВРЕМ
ИНФОРМАЦИОННАЯ ПРОГРА

# FIRST DETAILS OF
# SATELLITE TV IN UK

# NEW CHANNELS:
# SATELLITE AND CABLE

A S THE FIRST country in the world to develop a genuine public high-definition (as then defined) television service, Britain unsurprisingly led the world in cable television development. 'Piped' cable television of the in-building kind was pioneered in some luxury apartments in London during the late 1930s. Another pioneer cable development in Britain was the world's first wideband cable for expanding the country's television network. This was the London–Birmingham cable, opened in 1936, which was designed from the outset to carry both telephone calls and television. In the event its television use was only experimental and then only after the Second World War. Nevertheless, the cable and equipment performed very well – so well that a new television cable of greater capacity was installed for the opening of BBC Television's Birmingham transmitter in 1949.

Cable television as we know it today, delivering programmes to multiple households, took off in the 1950s. In those days, before the era of multi-channel programming, cable existed not as an alternative to broadcast television but as the sole means of providing watchable pictures to viewers who lived in what were called 'fringe areas'. These were the towns beyond the coverage of the television transmitters, and the 'logical' solution of relay or 'rebroadcast' relay transmitters was considered too expensive. Instead, a relay company would erect a receiving antenna on the highest hill nearby and pipe the signal to households on cable. Legislation enabling this to go ahead was passed in 1949 and within a year towns such as Gloucester and Northampton were enjoying the benefits of television previously denied to them. Another large installation served the Isle of Thanet.

By the 1970s multi-channel cable television was available in some towns and conurbations. A more specialised cable network on a grand scale operated in London in the 1970s. It was operated by the Inner London Education Authority and distributed educational television programmes from a central studio to schools across the capital. The big boost to cable came in 1983 when the government awarded eleven major new-build multi-channel franchises, all but one of which were operational by 1991. In that year cable operators

Opposite:
Public interest
in satellite
television was
aroused in 1981
when this colour
magazine appeared
in the shops. In
those days a very
substantial dish
and expensive
technical
equipment were
needed to receive
any programmes
from the skies.

# SATELLITE super station europe

gained full rights to offer their own telephone services. In 2008 the total number of subscribers to cable television in Britain was over 3.3 million and the United Kingdom's largest operator, Virgin Media, offered subscribers more than two hundred entertainment channels.

As up-to-the-minute as satellite television may seem, the idea dates back to October 1945. The notion was first proposed by Sir Arthur C. Clarke in that month's issue of *Wireless World* magazine, in which he set out a comprehensive specification for placing communications satellites hovering in space over the earth in geostationary orbit. With a devastating world war just over, few people took this seriously, an attitude that persisted until the Russians shocked the world in 1958 by launching Sputnik, the world's first artificial satellite.

The landmark year for satellite television was 1962, when the Telstar satellite was launched for the American Telephone and Telegraph Company (AT&T). Telstar was the first satellite to transmit television signals (and telephone calls) across the Atlantic, with earth stations in the United States, Britain and France. Unlike the geostationary satellites of today, Telstar did not orbit the earth; it needed complex tracking aerials and could not be 'seen' by an aerial looking at a fixed point in the sky. The first, rather formal link-up was on 23 July and satellite television's first scoop was in the following year, 1963, when the BBC relayed coverage live from America after the assassination of President Kennedy. The breakthrough event came in 1967 when the Beatles' 'All You Need Is Love' concert was broadcast worldwide by satellite to an audience of 150 million.

GOONHILLY DOWNS & SATELLITE COMMUNICATIONS GPO

Satellite television in those days enabled broadcasters to exchange programmes but was not intended for home viewing, not least because reception required a dish aerial 26 metres in diameter. The first step towards the direct-to-home satellite broadcasting of today came in 1975 when hobbyist Steve Birkill, then working at BBC TV's Holme Moss transmitter station, constructed the world's first home satellite receiver. Within a few years a dozen or so intrepid

enthusiasts had constructed dishes of around 6 metres in diameter to watch satellite programmes from the USSR – rather frugal fare, but the real pleasure was in the sense of achievement.

By now the public and the government were becoming satellite-minded, and in 1980 a Thames Television documentary about the future of television on satellite made an impact on many people. It certainly did on the programme's producer, Brian Haynes, who was so impressed with the concept that he resigned to set up a company that he called Satellite Television Ltd. With collaboration from British Telecom and an injection of capital, he managed to gain a slot on the OTS-2 orbiting test satellite under the guise of transmitting experimental broadcasts. His 'Satellite' station was launched in 1982, transmitting half an hour of programming in English every evening, and at first very few people had equipment to watch these programmes (or room for the 3-metre dish required). Gradually the viewing figures grew and so did the interest of the media mogul Rupert Murdoch, who bought the equity in Haynes's company and renamed it Sky Channel.

Until 1985 home viewing of satellite programmes had been technically illegal but in that year the British government relaxed the rules on private home dishes. Consumer interest took off steeply when in 1988 the Astra satellite was launched as the first mass-market European television satellite. Its higher power meant that viewers no longer required large dishes to receive satellite transmissions. Sky Channel now moved on to the Astra platform, the manufacturer Amstrad brought out low-cost satellite reception equipment, and satellite television began to take off in Europe. The advent of the rival station British Satellite Broadcasting in 1990 failed to dent the success of Sky and later that year the two stations merged to create a combined organisation known as British Sky Broadcasting, which remains to this day.

Left: Amateur satellite pioneer Hugh Cocks built this enormous dish in his back garden in the early 1980s. Measuring 6 metres in diameter, it was used to receive television programmes beamed at Morocco, Algeria, Sudan, Argentina and Brazil on 4GHz C-band microwave frequencies.

Below: British Satellite Broadcasting launched its ambitious five-channel offering in 1990 but failed to match the appeal of Sky Television. Later that year the two services merged to form BSkyB.

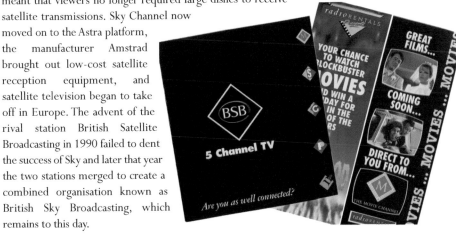

# FANTASTIC FAILURES

FOR OBVIOUS REASONS history focuses more on heroic success than ignominious failure. Nevertheless not every ambitious project has met success and a number of them failed spectacularly. Among these were Baird's 600-line colour television system, the single national transmitter, airborne television, pay television and the ITV station WWN.

Although television broadcasting in Britain ceased just before the outbreak of war in 1939, the television pioneer John Logie Baird continued technical research at his home laboratory. By the end of 1940 he had developed a colour television system with six hundred line definition along principles rather different from those of today. A scanning beam was passed through a rotating filter that had two transparent segments, one of red-orange colour and the other blue-green. The light reflected from the object being televised was picked up by photocells. A similar revolving filter was used in the receiver to produce colour images that were described as having 'a very fine quality'. The following year Baird refined this system to produce even better results but, despite this technical success, there was no application for colour television during wartime, especially for a system that was incompatible with 'standard' television equipment.

The single national television transmitter was a scheme hatched in the age of austerity that followed the Second World War. Despite the great pressure to extend the television service nationwide, finance for this was not forthcoming and in any case Britain's manufacturing and manpower resources could not

The first photograph of British colour television, taken off-screen under wartime conditions on 20 December 1940. The subject is the aviatrix Paddy Naismith, who had come to see the press demonstration of Baird's new colour television system.

have coped. Accordingly the Post Office (then responsible for broadcasting policy) devised in 1947 its own low-orbit geostationary satellites – aerials suspended from a constellation of six balloons tethered over the country at a height of 5,000 feet. It was acknowledged there were mechanical problems to be overcome from lightning, gales and ice, but these did not appear insuperable. The potential hazard to aircraft might have been more difficult to overcome but the scheme attracted careful consideration for a time.

The 1965 ban on cigarette advertising on ITV created a lucrative opportunity for the so-called 'pirate' offshore radio broadcasters to expand into television using transmitters aboard aeroplanes. The most ambitious project came from Radio Caroline, whose transmissions were due to start at 6 p.m. on 1 July 1970 on Channel 68 from a Super Constellation aircraft circling the North Sea at 20,000 feet. More than £1 million was claimed to have been put into the project, and £650,000 of advertising booked. A champagne party was held in London to launch the new station. There is doubt whether the plane did actually take off, but airborne television has been deployed successfully in the United States for schools broadcasting and in Vietnam for the US Forces.

Television Wales West and North is the only British independent television contractor to have failed. Its heraldic Welsh dragon emblem reflected the station's pride, which was to come before a fall in 1964.

Pay television was another flop. Four companies were granted licences for this in 1963 but it appears only Pay TV Ltd went on the air, which operated over the British Relay systems in London and Sheffield between 1966 and 1968. This was hardly a paying proposition but the company's application to expand was refused by the government of the day, which terminated their licence, resulting in a loss of over £1million for Pay TV Ltd.

Experiments followed with local television, including one in Wellingborough with about 4,500 subscribers. This started in March 1974 and finished about a year later. On average there were 9 hours of programmes per week, with half produced locally, at a total cost of £20,000. Other localities that experimented with local programming (on cable systems, not over the air) in the 1970s were Bristol, Greenwich, Sheffield and Swindon.

In 1981 a company called SelecTV operated an experimental pay TV service on cable in Milton Keynes, Northampton and Wellingborough but this too failed to prosper. Paying for premium channels is the norm today but historically viewers considered the cost of extra channels poor value for money.

The final failure is the only ITV company to go off the air through insolvency, Television Wales West and North. Its name indicates its service area, which in the 1960s had the lowest television ownership of all ITV areas. Advertising revenue was poor from the station's opening in 1962 and declined when the government forced the broadcaster to increase the quota of Welsh language programmes. Two years later the company collapsed and its franchise was taken over by the other Welsh ITV franchise to create an all-Wales service.

# RETRO TELEVISION TODAY

ATTITUDES TOWARDS TELEVISION have changed a lot. Until the 1980s it was dismissed by many as an ephemeral and rather low-brow form of entertainment, while broadcasters generally felt uneasy about screening their heritage of old programmes for fear that more 'sophisticated' audiences might ridicule their older output. The coming of Channel Four, new satellite stations and the rise of home video have all created an insatiable demand for programme material, while a more enlightened attitude in the media has conditioned us to appreciate old television in a positive manner.

Pioneer groups such as Wider TV Access and later Kaleidoscope proved there was a demand for viewing old programmes by arranging public screenings, while the opening of the Museum of the Moving Image (since closed and much missed) and the National Media Museum (still open) also made an interest in old television respectable. Today there is no shortage of books, societies and conventions devoted to old television. Archive recordings are screened on television occasionally and can be bought on DVD, while the BBC and the National Film and Television Archive have had success in tracking down 'lost' programmes and returning them to the archive. 'Kaleidoscope' and 'Missing, Believed Wiped' are the titles of annual conventions devoted to old television in general, while specialist groups hold their own events related to *Doctor Who* and other 'cult' programmes.

## SCREENINGS OF OLD PROGRAMMES

A recent technical development now opens the prospect of restoring many more old programmes to their original glory. Originally the cost of videotape was simply too expensive to use for archiving colour programmes, although many were preserved on black and white film. Using the latest technology BBC research staff have been experimenting with a process to scan film recordings at high-definition (HD) standard and then recreate the colour information electronically. The process looks very promising, making a large number of programmes from 1968 to 1974 capable of being brought back to full colour.

Opposite:
The Amberley Working Museum in Sussex has set out a superb display of old televisions and video recorders by building a replica television dealer's showroom.

Above: Working displays of old televisions – complete with their large V-shaped rabbit's ears portable antennae – can be seen regularly at historical displays and collectors' swapmeets. The set on the right is a small-screen 'kitchen set' sold by Ferguson in the 1960s; it has separate tuning knobs for VHF (405-line) and UHF (625-line) programmes – what might now be called 'future proofing'.

## COLLECTING AND RESTORING OLD TELEVISION SETS

This is an absorbing and not necessarily expensive hobby. Technical and safety considerations mean that only qualified people should handle electrical restoration. Even though there are no longer any transmissions on the 405-line standard, converters can be found to adapt these old televisions and videorecorders to work with modern programmes.

Above: A non-working television is only half a television, which is why a growing band of enthusiasts gain much satisfaction in restoring them to working order. An understanding of electronics and the risks of high voltage are essential but most faults are simple to repair and the parts are generally inexpensive. Membership of the British Vintage Wireless Society is highly recommended.

Top right: If you enjoy recreating room settings, or if your inclination is towards a retro lifestyle, an old television set can complement period room decor in a powerful way. Such accessories can be found at jumble sales or on eBay.

## TELEVISION MUSIC

There is a strong interest in old theme tunes, production and presentation music, whilst even test-card music has a keen following of its own. In the 1970s, for instance, ITV played popular and classical music from commercial albums, while the BBC played light music that was recorded specially for test-card performance. Because the BBC's music was not for sale in the shops, a cult following grew and CD albums of original test-card music have been released. Specialist groups (see 'Societies and Information Sources' below) exist to channel the interest in television music and allied matters such as the films shown for trade test transmission purposes in the early days of colour television in Britain.

Left: An intriguing development of the early 1990s was the Retrovisor 'Festival' colour television produced in homage to the classic Bush TV22 design of the 1950s. Manufactured as a limited edition product by Radiocraft Ltd, it is now more valuable than the original that inspired it.

Below: Britain's pioneer 405-line television system may be technically obsolete but the nostalgic appeal of the old technology is set to live on for many years to come. Museums and enthusiastic collectors will work together to ensure this, as seen in this display at the Vintage Wireless Museum in London.

## TELEVISION ARCHAEOLOGY

So poorly was the early history of television preserved that museums and archives are relying on the public to rediscover lost treasures. Regular screenings of old television programmes held at the British Film Institute in London are lost programmes on film that have been rediscovered, often by enthusiasts searching through attics and junk shops. The original Intermediate Film Process camera used by Baird in 1935–6 turned up in a cine collector's garage and it was indeed fortunate that this unique artefact was recognised by another collector and saved for the nation. Members of the Alexandra Palace Television Society (APTS) have been responsible for locating, identifying and ensuring the preservation of cine film from the formative years of the BBC Television Service, filmed before the Second World War by lighting engineer Desmond Campbell. In June 2001 APTS received a grant from the Royal Television Society to preserve 1,300 photographs of television productions from 1937 to 1951.

If you have a sense of purpose and plenty of space at home, you can build your own museum of broadcasting. All manner of old television sets can be had cheaply at boot fairs and charity shops and, if nicely restored and displayed, they will gain in value.

## AN AMBITIOUS PROJECT

The British Heritage Television Project is the latest organisation with the goal of re-establishing a television display at the birthplace of BBC Television, Alexandra Palace. The volunteer group behind this activity states that this 'television centre' could become a major resource, attracting visitors from far and wide. Their aim is to create interactive exhibits, examples of television technology down the ages, vintage-style programme-making, and perhaps even low-power 405-line transmissions on the original Channel 1. For this last purpose their technicians are restoring a BBC television transmitter of the 1950s back to operating condition. Their website is at www.405-line.tv

This historic apparatus, discovered in a cine enthusiast's garage, is now in the National Media Museum in Bradford. An amazing survival, it is the actual camera used in Baird's so-called 'Intermediate Film' television process in 1936 when the BBC launched electronic television. In those days programmes were provided in alternate weeks using Marconi-EMI or Baird equipment. The latter system used film taken by a cine camera, which was processed, developed and scanned electronically in less than a minute after shooting. Only one camera was ever built for this purpose and this lucky find is it.

# IMPORTANT DATES IN TELEVISION HISTORY

**1925** John Logie Baird makes the world's first public demonstration of television in Selfridge's department store, London.

**1926** Television Ltd (later known as Baird Television) receives the first licence in the world issued specifically for the transmission of television pictures.

**1928** The world's first transatlantic television transmission of live pictures, from amateur radio station G2KZ in Coulsdon, Surrey, received in New York.

**1929** Baird begins thirty-line transmissions over BBC airwaves (ended 1935).

**1936** The BBC opens the first public electronic television system in the world.

**1937** Electronic television starts in France, from the Eiffel Tower transmitter on 455 lines.

**1938** Electronic television starts in Germany (Berlin, 441 lines). Freak reception enables BBC television programmes from London to be seen

This unassuming-looking wooden construction found at a car boot sale in Dublin was recognised as the hulk of a very early mechanical television receiver of the early 1930s. Despite its scruffy appearance, it is a unique and valuable relic of the earliest days of television.

in the United States. Radio Corporation of America researchers in New York capture these on film, the world's oldest video recording.

**1939** RCA introduces electronic television in the United States, at the New York World's Fair (441 lines). Afterwards the outbreak of war puts an end to television broadcasting in Britain and most other countries. The Germans resume television broadcasting in occupied Paris and the British set up a monitoring station in Sussex to watch the programming.

**1946** Television reopens in London.

**1949** The first provincial transmitter in Britain (Sutton Coldfield, serving the Midlands).

**1950** The first television outside broadcast from the Continent (*Calais en Fête*).

**1951** Bing Crosby Enterprises in California demonstrate the first professional video recorder, using tape moving at 100 inches per second.

**1953** Coronation ceremony televised in Britain and relayed to western Europe by Eurovision.

**1954** First full Eurovision link-up; eight countries take part.

**1955** BBC commences experimental colour transmissions (405 lines, American NTSC colour process). Commercial ('Independent') television (ITV) opens, but in the London area only.

**1956** ITV extended to the Midlands and north regions. Ampex launches a professional videotape recording machine that is rapidly adopted by many broadcasters.

**1957** ITV opens in Scotland. The 'Toddlers' Truce', an hour-long gap in programming between 6 and 7 p.m. to allow mothers to put children to bed, ends.

**1958** ITV reaches south Wales, the west and southern England.

**1959** ITV is extended to north-east England, Northern Ireland and the east of England. Toshiba in Japan introduces the helical scan system of videotape recording, the tape running at 15 inches per second.

**1960** ITV opens in south-east England.

**1961** ITV expands into south-west England, north-east Scotland and the Borders.

**1962** British viewers see the first live pictures from the United States, via the Telstar satellite. ITV moves into north and west Wales and the Channel Isles, becoming available to 96 per cent of the population.

**1964** BBC2 opens on 625 lines. The first (and only) failure of an ITV company: Wales West and North (WWN) taken over by Television Wales and West (TWW).

**1965** Cigarette commercials banned on ITV.

**1967** Regular colour transmissions start on BBC2.

**1968** Major reorganisation of ITV franchises brings in Thames, Yorkshire, Harlech and London Weekend Television. Rediffusion and ABC merge to create Thames.

**1969** Colour television introduced on ITV and BBC1. Sony Corporation produces its first colour cassette video recorder (non-domestic). Live pictures of men on the moon.

**1972** Launch of the Video Cassette Recorder by Philips, the first truly domestic machine. Independent Television Authority (ITA) becomes the Independent Broadcasting Authority (IBA).

**1975** First regular teletext broadcasts. The Japanese enter the home video market with VHS and Beta systems.

**1980** Most ITV contracts are renewed, but Southern TV and Westward TV are replaced by TVS and TSW. ATV is restructured and is renamed Central Independent TV.

**1982** Launch of Europe's first satellite channel, Satellite Television Ltd, later renamed Sky Channel. The BBC and ITV close down their 405-line networks. Viewers must now watch in 625 lines only.

**1989** Sky television launches a four-channel service using the Astra satellite.

**1990** British Satellite Broadcasting (BSB), the United Kingdom's official direct-to-home satellite television service opens. Unable to compete with Sky Television, it merges with its rival under the title British Sky Broadcasting.

# FURTHER READING

All of these books were available through amazon.co.uk at the time of writing.

Bennett-Levy, M. *Historic Televisions and Video Recorders*. Self-published, 1993. Large colour illustrated paperback.

Bennett-Levy, M. *TV Is King*. Self-published, 1994. More sumptuous colour illustrations; the sequel to *Historic Televisions and Video Recorders*.

Cornell, P., Day, M., and Topping, K. *The Guinness Book of Classic British TV*. Guinness Books, 1996. Substantial in-depth study of over one hundred classic and well-loved programmes.

Currie, A. *A Concise History of British Television 1930–2000*. Kelly Books, 2004. Accessible text, packed with information.

Emmerson, A. *Electronic Classics: Collecting, Restoring and Repair*. Newnes, 1998. Thick paperback packed with hard-to-find information on making old treasures work again.

Howett, D. *Television Innovations: 50 Technological Developments*. Kelly Books, 2006. Extensive paperback on the advances that made television a reality.

Kingsley, H., and Tibballs, G. *Box of Delights*. Macmillan, 1990. Masterpiece research combined with gifted, sympathetic writing, covering the 1950s to the 1980s. Programmes, personalities and even favourite commercials are all included, plus a 'Where are they now?' section.

Lazell, D. *What's on the Box?* This England, 1996. An engaging history of television viewing from early times to modern.

Tibballs, G., and Morris, Johnny. *Golden Age of Children's Television*. Titan Books, 1991. Large-format paperback covering the years 1950 to 1975; difficult to fault.

Vahimagi, T. *British Television*. Oxford University Press, 1996. Large illustrated paperback with detailed entries on more than 1,100 favourite television programmes from 1936 to the present.

Many sets were produced as combined television and radio receivers, as seen on this magazine cover. Sets were expensive and a high-performance all-wave radio helped justify the substantial cost.

# SOCIETIES AND INFORMATION SOURCES

Please send a stamped addressed envelope with all enquiries.

*Alexandra Palace Television Society*. Website: www.apts.org.uk APTS has been responsible for locating, identifying and ensuring the preservation of photographs, drawings and reminiscences concerning the Alexandra Palace studios and transmitters. The APTS Archive holds five thousand items in total.

*Alexandra Palace Television Trust*. Website:www.cix.co.uk/~joc/aptvt The trust is dedicated to restoring the old BBC studios and opening them to the public.

*British Film Institute / National Film and Television Archive*. Television programme database at www.bfi.org.uk/filmtvinfo/ftvdb Is it on DVD or video? www.bfi.org.uk/filmtvinfo/onvideo.html Occasionally the BFI screens old television programmes. Details at www.bfi.org.uk/whatson

*British Heritage Television Project*. Website: www.405-line.tv Aims to reopen the original television wing at Alexandra Palace as a display centre where the story of British television would be told. There might be interactive exhibits, examples of television technology down the ages, vintage-style programme-making and perhaps even 405-line transmissions on the original Channel 1.

*British Vintage Wireless Society*, 26 Castleton Road, Swindon SN5 5GD. Telephone: 01793 886062. Website: www.bvws.org.uk Many television collectors belong to BVWS, which often has articles on vintage television in its magazine.

*Kaleidoscope*. Website: k2k1.kaleidoscope.org.uk This is a voluntary, non-profit-making organisation devoted to the appreciation of classic and vintage British television. The group has staged many television festivals and retrospectives and publishes a unique range of reference books on old programming.

*Narrow Bandwidth Television Association*, 1 Sunny Hill, Milford, Derbyshire DE56 0QR. Website: www.nbtv.wyenet.co.uk The NBTVA newsletter covers Baird-era topics from time to time.

*Robert Farnon Society*, 33 Bramleys, Rochford, Essex SS4 3BD. Website: www.rfsoc.org.uk This thriving and long-established society is devoted to light music in all its forms, including television signature themes, production music and the like.

*Test Card Circle*, 175 Kingsknowe Road North, Edinburgh EH14 2DY. Website: www.testcardcircle.org.uk Publishes a regular magazine full of articles on test-card music and trade test films.

*Test Card Club*, 7 Epping Close, Derby DE3 4HR. Website: www.test-cards.fsnet.co.uk Quarterly magazine on test-card-related topics.

*Vintage Television, incorporating 405 Alive*. Website: www.bvws.org.uk/405alive/index.html The only magazine in the world devoted to the vintage television hobby in all its forms, now incorporated in the BVWS Bulletin.

# PLACES TO VISIT

It is advisable to telephone to check the opening times before making a journey to visit any of these attractions.

*Amberley Working Museum*, Amberley, Arundel, Sussex BN18 9LT. Telephone: 01798 831370. Website: www.amberleymuseum.co.uk In the Chalk Pits opposite Amberley station, with easy road access. Comprehensive industrial archaeology museum, with a superb selection of old television sets in a reconstructed radio and television showroom of the 1950s.

*The Bakelite Museum*, Orchard Mill, Williton, Somerset TA4 4NS. Telephone: 01984 632133. Website: www.bakelitemuseum.co.uk/index.htm A unique display of vintage plastics and domestic items (including old televisions) set within a seventeenth-century watermill.

*Design Museum*, 28 Shad Thames, London SE1 2YD. Telephone: 020 7403 6933. Website: www.designmuseum.org A small number of design classic sets are on show.

*Museum of Science and Industry*, Liverpool Road, Castlefield, Manchester M3 4JP. Telephone: 0161 832 2244. Website: www.msim.org.uk/explore-mosi/communications/radio-and-television Fascinating broadcasting gallery.

*National Media Museum* (formerly the Museum of Photography, Film and Television), Prince's View, Bradford BD1 1NQ. Telephone: 01274 727488. Website: www.nmpft.org.uk/home.asp Good displays of old television cameras and receivers. The Television Heaven exhibit allows visitors to enter a 'time capsule' and recapture the impression of television viewing in the past.

*National Wireless and Television Museum*, The High Lighthouse, Harwich, Essex. Telephone: 07971 766808. Website: www.nvwm.freeservers.com An interesting display that is well worth visiting but not as elaborate as the title might suggest.

*Science Museum*, Exhibition Road, South Kensington, London SW7 2DD. Telephone: 0870 870 4868. Website: www.sciencemuseum.org.uk Broadcast communications gallery with many interesting exhibits (plus many other items in store).

*Vintage Wireless Museum*, West Dulwich, London SE21. Telephone: 020 8670 3667. Website: bvwm.org.uk Delightful museum with working pre-war television sets and ex-BBC standard converters. Often featured on television. Visitors must telephone first for an appointment.

*York Castle Museum*, The Eye of York, York YO1 1RY. Telephone: 01904 653611. Website: www.yorkcastlemuseum.org.uk Exhibits include 1950s living room and a Bush TV22 set on which you can watch *Hancock's Half Hour*.

COLLECTORS' FAIR

*National Vintage Communications Fair*. Website: www.nvcf.org.uk/ Organised by the British Vintage Wireless Society and held annually at the Warwickshire Exhibition Centre.

# INDEX

Printed and bound by CPI Group (UK) Ltd, Croydon, CR0 4YY

20/05/2022

03124711-0006